Copyright © 2019 by Christie L. Starkweather

All rights reserved.

No part of this book may be reproduced in any form or by any electronic or mechanical means including information storage and retrieval systems, without permission in writing from the author, with exception to book reviews or articles written about the book and /or author.

Christie L. Starkweather

Visit me on Facebook:
facebook.com/clspoetry
CLSPoetry by Christie Starkweather

and at

clspoetry
on Instagram

ISBN
9781791785390

Cover design by Amanda Coleman
www.amandaxcoleman.com
www.facebook.com/a.x.cdesignservices/

From The Ashes

A collection of
Poetry
&
Prose

Written By

Christie L. Starkweather

FROM THE ASHES

From the Ashes

I am born from the ashes
Of trials and defeat
Built from the many wounds
That have refused to bleed
My soul has been bruised
Defiled and burned
These wings now forsaken
Have become tattered and torn
But these smoldering feathers
Do not define who I am
And from my bloodied knees
Still I'll rise and I'll stand
So break me and scar me
Set my soul ablaze to burn
And from the dusty ashes
I will rise again reborn.

Chapter 1: The Dark of Hell

The Dark of Hell digs into the deepest, darkest places of the mind, tearing at the fears of the darkness and of being devoured by our demons, of loneliness, rejection and abandonment. Every soul holds a dark place where fear drowns hope and the Devil imprisons the mind.

Chapter 2: Fire to Ash

Fire to Ash explores the state of sorrow and depression, of heartache and frustration, of anger and of hate, and all that can be broken within the heart, mind, body and soul.

Chapter 3: Lost in Madness

Lost in madness is a brief tribute to Wonderland and the thought we all have a touch of madness in our hearts and wonder in our souls.

Chapter 4: Finding Peace

Finding Peace takes us on a journey to a freedom from fear and sadness. It travels through the hope of love, inspiration and motivation of a better day.

Chapter 5: Resurrection

Resurrection is the renewal of faith and strength. It is the beauty of the rising phoenix, learning to fly once again. The end of one life and the beginning of another.

The Dark of Hell

Of Skeletons & Monsters

There are skeletons in my closet
And monsters beneath my bed
Many dark secrets are hidden
Behind the demons in my head
And though I should let them go
Denying them another thought
They were always there for me
In the moments when you were not.

Forgotten

How tragic the lonely smile
Of a forgotten girl
Having so much to give
That no one wants to have.

Dying Embers

My fire has burned out, leaving little more than luke warm cinders
and ashes blowing in the wind. Slowly, I fade away into the
cold and unforgiving darkness that I have come to know as home;
holding tightly to the last flickering flame of hope
that you will find me here and reignite the embers of my soul.

Deceptive are the mighty gates of Hell,
as it is an angel who stands beyond the doorway.

Condemnation

I thought you were my everything.
Perfection come to save me.
My hope. My light in the dark.
But every candle burns out
And turns to smoldering ash.
You bent me, bruised me, broke me,
Forever scarring my soul.
You decimated the last
Sliver of hope left in me,
Leaving me broken and kneeling
To the torments of my hell.
When all I wanted from you
Was for you to just love me,
But instead, you took everything
And condemned me to despair.

I never knew how sadistic your demons were
until they made mine cry.

Inferno

Buried in my thoughts and haunted by my past
The world passes by and I don't even glance
Seeking out redemption for the Hell within my soul
I'm lost deep within myself with nowhere left to go
So I'll bury myself deeper until I can find my way
Out of this dark inferno and into the light of day.

The Mask of Regret

My soul hides among those of the dead,
married to death himself. Relentlessly, I shall
continue my attempts to claw my way out of Hell,
casting away the mask that has kept me bound and
imprisoned within the fires of regret.

Sorrowful Days

I've been broken and bruised
I've been brought to my knees
I've begged to the Heavens
End this suffering please
Heal all that's damaged
And please let me move on
Let these sorrowful days
Be forgotten and gone.

Devil at the Door

I really should have known better
Than to believe your many lies
I thought I truly meant something
But to you I was just a prize
I can't believe I fell for you
Or let you make me cry
The Devil he rang my doorbell
And sure enough I did reply.

Potential

I saw in you the potential for the Heaven
That I fought my way through Hell for
But instead you became
Just another demon standing in the way.

Oubliette

My shattered heart
Bitter, tainted, hollow
Full of torment, remorse, despair
Trapped in this oubliette
Forgotten, alone, desiccating
Yet I see you through the darkness
Bright, vivid, illuminating
And I think maybe
Just maybe
You might be the one to save me
And breathe life back in this lifeless soul.

Secrets

Only God knows the secrets
I keep hidden in the dark
He knows why I look away
At such a harmless remark
He knows the tears I cried alone
Just to spare you from the pain
He alone knows the storm I fared
To keep you sheltered from the rain
He gave me strength to carry on
And to find solace in today
And to put the past behind me
Where my secrets shall remain.

*Perhaps our demons keep us awake at night
because they too cannot bare the thought of being alone.*

Deception

With fire in her eyes and magic in her soul
She'll bring you to your knees and never let you go
She'll mesmerize your mind and keep you in her hold
Unknowingly you signed and to the Devil you were sold.

*Darkness herself weeps for my suffering
As even she is helpless
In saving me from my own torment.*

Break Free

I've been buried in my lies
And smothered by my guilt
I've hidden long enough
Behind these walls that I've built
I'm going to break these chains
And I am going to break free
To exorcise these demons
And get them out of me.

*Being broken isn't what hurts.
It's the fact that no one noticed
You were breaking in the first place.*

Tourniquet

I wish I could shake this emptiness.
This feeling that something is very wrong
But I just can't seem to figure out what it is.
It's like my soul itself is torn and bleeding.
Hemorrhaging.
Leaving me weak and wondering
If I'm going to bleed out on the floor.
I'd put a tourniquet on it if I could,
Just to stop it,
But I think the wounds are just too deep
And the damage is already done.

Demons

My demons will
Always be a
Part of me
Tugging
Pulling
Trying to
Contain me
Hold me
Suppress me
I cannot stop that
But I am
And will always be
Stronger than them.

The Understanding

I sit in quiet contemplation
And reflection of what went wrong
To gain an understanding
Of where it is that I belong
I have depths too deep to dive
And walls too high to climb
And secrets buried way beneath
The unforgiving sands of time
There's things you don't know about me
That I couldn't trust to share
Hidden well within a tangled web
Of my deepest and darkest fears
My demons love to whisper
And place doubts upon my heart
They feast upon my weaknesses
So that I might fall apart
But my heart's as strong as mountains
And as relentless as the seas
Still as vibrant as the sunset
And full of generosities
My soul is still kind and gentle
Even after all that I've been through
But my demons did convince me
I wasn't good enough for you
And so I watched you walk away
And refused to put up a fight
I couldn't help but wonder
What if the Devil might be right
So I gained the understanding
Of exactly what went wrong
I forgot for just a moment
There's simply no place where I belong.

Judgment

Those fires of Hell
Are burning my heels
I tried to outrun them
But the demons have caught up
And I don't have the strength
To keep on running away
It's impossible to escape
The inevitable damnation
And I cannot continue this fight
So I'm submitting myself
To the consequences of
Trying to run from the Devil
Yes, the last little bit of hope
Has finally melted away
Leaving scars on the only
Undamaged place left in my heart
And all my tears feel like acid rain
Burning as they stream down my cheek
As I make my way back through
The dark, twisted gates of Hell
To face my final judgment.

Fallen From Grace

I feel the chilling breath upon my neck
As the bony fingers of Death shall beck
And the sirens will sing me to my grave
For this soul of mine cannot be saved
And so, I'll walk through Hell's fiery gates
Another angel, fallen from grace.

Sometimes the brightest souls
Are the ones harboring the darkest demons.

Redemption

I sought redemption
In the fires of Hell
But the Devil cast me out
So I sought redemption
In the Holy Light
But the angels turned me down
And so I walked the world alone
Condemned to my
Eternal isolation
Seeking within myself
A redemption that
Was unobtainable
For a soul that neither
Demons nor angels
Were willing to embrace.

Your Memory

The thoughts of you
Run up my spine
Creeping
Crawling
Into my mind
Twisting
Turning
Poisoning me
Forever imprisoned
By your memory.

*You can never truly defeat your demons,
but you can learn to stay ahead of them.*

Life Lesson #1

The cruelest lesson
Life ever taught me,
No one is coming
To save you.

Shrapnel

You won't find a shred
Of balance within me
And synchronicity is
Nowhere to be found
Within my dictionary
I'm a chaotic mess
The train wrecked result
Of two rollercoasters
Colliding together
Buried deep in the debris and
Bleeding out from the shrapnel
Just struggling to breath
So do not look for peace here
The best I can do is to pull
A twisted, mangled piece of metal
From my heart to give you
A memento of the spoils of war
Between reality and the struggle
To become something better.

Whisper

There's a quietness in my soul
Of an unfamiliar silence
The subtle moment of peace
My heart has yearned so long for
Speak gently if you must
A somber, hushed whisper
For my demons are sleeping
And I dare not wake them.

Pits of Hell

I'm holding on for dear life
One loose finger away from plummeting
Into my own personal Hell
Desperately searching for anything
That can sustain me for just a little while longer
I see you staring down at me
Placing your judgment upon me
For deeds you cannot understand
Baring down that final blow of guilt
That sends me barreling towards
The depths of darkness that I so feared
I take comfort though in knowing
That someday judgment will come for you
And you'll find me waiting
In the pits of Hell
A smile on my face and
A sign in my hand that reads
'Welcome Home, Asshole!'

Shadows of Self Deceit

She found comfort in the
Catacombs of Hell
Where madness roams free
Playing hide and seek
With demons
Allowing just a few moments
Here and there
To relinquish the burdens
Of meeting the expectations
Of normalcy
How tragic the need
To hide our true selves
Within the shadows
Of self deceit.

Darkness Comes

When darkness comes
To collect his toll
He'll rise from Hell
To steal your soul
His bony fingers
Reaching in
To devour it all
With a side of sin
Leaving the shell
That you'll become
As none can hide
When darkness comes.

Silence

I drowned my demons
In all the tears
That I cried over you
Now, not even they
Can be saved
And everything
Has gone silent.

Take These Wings

I had my chance to fly
And yet, all I found
Were empty blue skies
And a thousand broken dreams
Drifting through the clouds
So please, take these wings
Maybe you'll find Heaven
Where I could not.

Insomnia

I'm not haunted by what was
It's the thoughts of what
Could have been, should have been
That plagues my mind at night
When the roads not taken
Turn into one way detours
To condemnation and regret
And the insomnia is all
I have left to remember you by.

Salvation

Your ghost lingers in
The corners of my mind
Haunting me
Taunting me
Twisting my thoughts
Until even my demons
Had been driven mad
Begging for salvation
From the memory of you.

Tempting Fate

I tried to outrun my demons
But they cannot be outran
I tried to get away from you
But around each corner you'd stand
I tried to cast away the Devil
But he loves to have his fun
I tried to stay inside the light
But darkness always comes
I tried to forget my past
And all of my mistakes
Lord knows how much I tried
But I only tempted fate.

Hell's Ashes

The most beautiful soul
Came not from the stars
It rose from Hell's ashes
Born from her scars.

Muddied Waters

I've danced with the Devil
And my demons within
I've drowned my very soul
In the murky, muddied waters of sin
I've served up my heart
Feeding the monsters of my past
Trying to hold on to what
My fingers could not grasp
But not once did I regret
A single fire that I lit
Because in the end I'll smile
And never say what if.

A Million Souls

A million souls cry out in the the night
So much burden for one tiny world
Screams of heartache and pain
Ringing through the Heavens
A million souls reaching out
Begging for console
Pleading for solace
Trying to hold on to hope
That somebody is listening
A million souls sit in silence
Alone. Waiting. Broken.

Darkness Blooms

Casting its veil of shadows
Darkness blooms in tragedy
As the forgotten are forsaken
In the wake of hypocrisy.

Carnival

Round and round this carnival of night
The rollercoaster freakshow of my life
Unable to escape this nightmarish Hell
Trapped upon the Devil's carousel
Endless circles within my mind
A funhouse maze, it twists and winds
Round and round the carousel goes
An endless ticket to the
Carnival of Souls.

Hellfire

With a soul that burns of fire
She walks through Hell unscathed
Burning everything to ashes
That's standing in her way.

What Ifs

There are no monsters
Hiding under my bed
Just the ghosts of my past
Haunting me with my what ifs.

Warrior Scars

Wounded wings refuse to heal
Long after war was waged
Broken, battered, bleeding out
Yet I ask not to be saved
Though weary boned, I'll prevail
A warrior's scars inscribed
A worthy price for freedom
In the battle to survive.

Death of a Butterfly

I remember my soul
Being beautiful
And vividly bright
Like wings of a butterfly
But its magnificent color
Faded away in the darkness
So broken and alone
Crumbling, decaying
As it lays itself to rest
Where butterflies go to die.

Wolves do not bow to sheep
Even when their hearts
Are bigger than their teeth.

Kiss of Death

She welcomed the kiss of Death
With open arms
As Death had been the only one
That had ever meant to keep her.

I'm Trying

When I flinch at your touch
And push against your embrace
Please understand
The demons I face
And it's not that I don't want
You to hold me at night
It's that the last one I loved
Never loved me quite right
Their touch was not gentle
Their embrace was not warm
They left my soul broken
As my body bled on the floor
But I'm trying
Dear god am I trying
To just let you in
And open my heart
To loving somebody again.

The Devil & A Dragon

Do not look to her
To quench the fires
Burning within your soul
For she has walked
Through Hell's corridors
And dined with
The Devil himself
She has a dragon spirit
And will not hesitate
To eat you alive.

Blackbird

A quiet flutter in the air
A somber whisper doth declare
That on this night the Blackbird flies
Beckoned by these sorrowed cries
To take my soul where it may rest
And release these burdens from upon my chest
And release these worries from upon my soul
For to the Ferry Man, I've paid my toll
So come now, Blackbird, my old friend
And on this night, your wings shall lend
To carry me high, to Heaven's door
For here my soul belongs no more.

Fire to Ash

Forgive Us

Celestial tears fall from Heaven
The moon cries for our suffering
Where is Eden when we need it
God cries for our mistakes
We have failed him
Father forgive us for we are impure
We know evil
We live Chaos
We cannot stop the bleeding
We have killed the world
And so I weep.

Tornado

You were a tornado to my heart.
Beautiful at a distance,
Powerful and unstoppable.
Breathtaking really.
I was pulled to you as
You drew ever so close.
Before I knew it,
You had consumed me
And it was too late.
The damage was done
And you were gone,
Leaving nothing but
Eradicated shards
Of who I used to be
Trapped beneath shattered
Walls that I once called home.

Abyss

My heart is as vast and deep as the ocean
A whole other world no one has ever seen
And can only be found if you aren't afraid
To swim the darkened abyss of my mind.

                Hold your breath.
                    It's a very long
                        Way down.

Round and Round

Round and round we go again
In this circle of deceit
Lies start flooding in again
Like a song that's on repeat
You tell me once more you love me
And then, once more, you walk away
I'm getting so sick and tired
Of these games you like to play
My head is getting dizzy
From all these mind tricks that you do
This record's gotten all worn out
And I've had enough of you.

I was finally able to quiet my mind only to realize
It was my heart all along that was screaming.

Halo

I see through your halo
Made of stained glass
Knowing someday it will fall
Shattering at your feet
Where everyone will see your lies
Among the reflections of truths
Which lay upon the floor.

Price to Pay

My heart and head are so messed up
Over the thought of losing you
I cry myself to sleep each night
Not knowing what to do
I wasn't supposed to fall so hard
And tried to keep my feelings at bay
I wish to God I'd known
Just how steep the price I'd pay.

Eye of the Storm

You thought you were through the storm,
But you're only in the calm of it.
      Hold on tight.
          It's not done
                With you yet.

*I'm not afraid of you loving me.
I'm afraid that you'll let go
And decide that you don't.*

Trojan Horse

You lied, deceived, declared war on my heart
And like the Trojan horse
You manipulated your way inside
And burned everything I am to the ground.

Mourning Fog

I hate that empty feeling that washes over you like a dense fog rolling across an open field, isolating you from everyone and everything. You don't know where it came from or how long it will continue to roll across. All you know is that it surrounded you, engulfed you, with a sense of voidness. An unimaginable emptiness that cannot be defined. You aren't even sure what you're missing, but you feel an overwhelming need to mourn for it. And you cannot stop it from rolling over you. You can only wait it out until the fog is ready to lift. So here I sit, patiently waiting, because it's too thick to see my way through.

Sands of Time

He didn't know how beautiful he was to me.
How every time I saw him, I trembled
And wanted to fall to my knees.
How the sands of time would stop pouring
Just to dance around him in a whirlwind.
He didn't know how his smile extinguished
Every ounce of sorrow that I'd held for so long.
And he never knew how much he meant to me
Because I never found the words to tell him
Before someone else brought him to his knees.
Now the sands of time dance for her
As they bury me in regret.

Wildfire

She has conviction in her words
And she has fire in her soul
Untamable
Unstoppable
Raging beyond control
Her candor is forthcoming
Her persistence is immense
Her mere presence will consume you
As her flames grow more intense
You cannot quench her passion
Her resolution will not sway
This wildfire will burn everything
That is standing in her way.

Shattered Dreams

My shattered dreams and shattered past
Mixed among shards of broken glass
So maliciously laid down at my feet
By demons I have yet to defeat
And I try not to scream in pain
As I walk this broken road again
The blood stained ground now painted red
And endless nightmares in my head
Of my shattered dreams and shattered past
Mixed among shards of broken glass
Forever playing itself on repeat
As I am finally forced to claim defeat
And though I tried I cannot wake
Until I atone for my mistakes.

Silly Little Fairytales

I recall how, in my childhood, on rainy days, I'd sit on the porch and read, oh so many stories and fairytales. I dreamt of being rescued from my tower of imprisonment. I held on to that dream for so long because it was such a beautiful thought that someone would fight their way through the fires of Hell just for me. But a day came when the dreams stopped coming, and I awoke to realize that they had been nothing more than the silly little dreams of a silly little girl who read a silly little fairytale. And how silly of me was it to believe anyone wanted to save me? Now I fear the time has passed for me to even save myself.

Beautiful Lie

You were the most beautiful lie I ever fed myself,
But I was always left hungry for more
As I fed upon your empty words and hollow promises,
When in truth, every time I fed on that lie,
I was starving my soul to its death.

Ashes and Dust

She loved with the fierceness of a thousand suns
And none dared to embrace the flames
And so the flames embraced her
Consumed her
Until they burned clear through
Destroying the soul
They all feared to touch
Leaving a broken shell
Of ashes and dust.

Numb

Those who have loved too much
And been loved too little
Become the ones who
No longer feel too much
But rather
Beg to feel anything at all
I just want to feel anything
Anything at all.

Sorrow's Silence

Sorrow's silence, bent and broken
Painful truths left unspoken
Shattered dreams and distant cries
Hide beneath the many lies
Quiet whispers remain unheard
The truths of love and hate and war
All the secrets that are contained
Cause the innocent to be blamed
Broken hearts void of emotion
Build the pain until explosion
Too quickly time will set the sun
Everything you know will be gone
Speak the truths with all their pain
Fear not the falling of the rain
Broken hearts will someday heal
You cannot stop what it is you feel
The sun will set and stars will fade
How will you live your life today.

Weary Soul

My soul has become weary
Stretched as thin as the
Tear stained parchment paper
That my anguished words
Have become smeared across
Stretching more and more
With each passing day
And I have to wonder
How much more can I take
Before it all tears me apart.

Sinful Heart

She was a sinful heart with hardened veins
A burning soul with a fiery gaze
Imprisoned within her deepest fears
And drowning in her sorrowed tears
Longing for a soft embrace
A gentler touch upon her face
So hold her close if you can
And you'll find forever hand in hand.

Fading Dreams

Once upon a fleeting dream
Shooting stars kissed the moon
And eternity rested upon
These forsaken lips
With the oh, so sweet taste
Of honey whiskey sunsets
Endless golden sunrises
And waking next to you
But as this dream slowly fades
So, too, do my memories of you
As eternity is once again defeated
By the unrelenting sands of time.

*I wanted to remember that moment forever,
but what I wouldn't give now,
just to forget.*

Finding Home

Twisted truths and broken hearts
Tired dreams of humble starts
Innocence lost at every bend
And a bruised soul just trying to mend
Shadows lurking in my mind
Of everything that was left behind
And in the wake of shattered trust
Faith and hope have turned to dust
So where then do you turn
When all your scars begin to burn
And you cannot see beyond lonely tears
Or escape haunting memories of your fears
Your weary mind begging to just let go
Of silly thoughts of ever finding home
Such a silly thought of ever finding home
When all you find is yourself alone.

Crashing Waves

Like the waves that violently
Crash against the rocky shore
Memories of you relentlessly beat
Against my hardening heart
Slowly carving away
At what remains
Carrying pieces of me
Far out to sea
One by one
Until all that's left
Is the bare foundation
Upon which I must learn
To rebuild once again.

3:28 am

3:28 in the morning
Laying there, missing you
Aching for your touch
Your gentle kiss upon my cheek
The warmth of you beside me
And in the darkness, I reach
Hoping it was only a dream
Finding only tear soaked sheets
And the memory of where
You were supposed to be.

*It was so easy for you to say goodbye,
That I wish I had never said hello.*

Cold Blooded

The bitter words slid off your tongue
Like a snake slithering through the grass
Your venomous bite stung like Hell
And I thought for certain
The poison would kill me
I still carry the puncture wounds on my heart
Reminding me every day
The consequences of falling for someone
As cold blooded as you.

Never Again

She knew she couldn't trust herself
To be left alone with him
How many times she'd told herself
Never. Ever. No, never again
But there was just something about him
That had crept under her skin
It coursed through her veins
With lustful addiction
And with each soft touch and gentle kiss
She'd fall slowly into submission
Giving into the temptation
Until never, ever, became
Once more again.

Sweet Dreams

She spent her life dancing in the clouds
A dreamer
A lover
A believer
Swaying to the song of her heart
Dancing to the rhythm of life
Tonight, she dances with the angels
One final act to a goodnight lullaby
Sweet dreams, my darling
My dancer of the stars
Sweet dreams.

The Magician

You were the master of all lies
Selling your illusions of love
With trickery and with deceit
Offering the perception of dreams
Within a bottle of lust, to see
Who would dance with the Devil
And dance with you they did
All as you picked their pockets
Stealing their last bits of hope
That happiness might still exist
Then as the dawn approaches
You vanish without a trace
Taking your illusions of love
And leaving empty promises
And heartache in your wake.

Heavenly Sin

Love left the sweetest taste
Lingering upon crimson lips
Begging to be washed away
With your gentle kiss
Your gentle touch
Your strong embrace
To feel your breath
Upon my face
And if tomorrow comes
You're gone again
My lips will still taste
Of heavenly sin.

Our Story

Our story was not written for books.
We had to salvage it from the wars
Our hearts fought against each other.
We tore it from the gnashing jaws
Of our controlling, selfish demons,
Determined to keep it for themselves.
Our story was written in the scars
That we etched across each others souls.
It was never a beautiful story, but it was ours,
And no stronger love could ever be found.

Playing Pretend

We all played pretend as children
Yet here we are, now grown
Still pretending
Pretending we don't give a damn
Pretending that we do
Pretending we don't love them
Pretending that they do
Pretending it's all okay
Pretending we're just fine
Just wishing we could go back
To simpler childhood times
Just sitting with our friends
All day, while we play pretend.

Heart of Misery

You can have your
Lying, cheating, sorry
Heart of misery
But darling
You burned the bridge
So I burned the memories.

Graffitied Hearts

We painted pictures of love upon a society
Where going through the motions
Became every day life
Where our lack of self worth
Eats away at iron souls
Rusting from the inside out
Turning our graffitied hearts
Into dust beneath our feet
Walked upon without regret.

Wildflower

She was the wildflower blooming at night
Growing in darkness, starving for light
Craving his touch and his heart's yearn
But he was too afraid of touching her thorns.

Midnight

He was the darkness
That crept beneath my skin
Seeping deep into the
Cracks of my bones
Leaving me wishing
Begging and pleading
That midnight would last
For eternity.

Etchings of Loneliness

I know what she did to you. What they all did. They didn't just break your heart, They consumed it. Consumed you. They etched loneliness into your soul until you believed that was all there was left. But you are not alone and my heart is not one to be feared. So I will lay beside you in the darkness until you no longer fear it, or me. And your heart, don't worry, I've given you mine, for it loves you enough to heal us both.

Hidden

She covered all the parts of her
That she feared to be seen
Hiding her heart, her soul
And everything
In between.

Her heart hungers for something real,
while her soul slowly starves to death.

The Feeling of Real

I have yet to experience the feeling of real
I have felt fake love in nights of convenience
And false friendships within the burning scars upon my back
I have known bucketfuls of empty promises
That have been poured mercilessly down my throat
Drowning the possibilities of knowing any real hope
The only real I know is the 3am loneliness
Where I pretend to be loved by someone
Who was never even really there.
Hell, I'm not even sure
If I'm real anymore.

Unworthy

So little thought given
To the damage suffered
Using
Abusing
Breaking hearts
No wonder so many of us
Feel unworthy of love.

Missing Me

I've been missing me
For some time now
And I'm not sure
Where I've gone
But I'm really
Starting to wonder
If I'm ever
Coming home.

Harbored Memories

Everything that
Once was broken
Can be repaired
But never again
Will it be the same
As the tears
Will always seep
Between the cracks
Etched by memories
Of harbored pain.

Vulnerability

It frightened him
How much he needed her
Yet at the same time
There was a comfort
In the arms of vulnerability
And an undeniable truth
That forever
Might just be possible.

Unheard

My heart cries out
Like a sad song
Drifting on the wind
Desperate to be heard
Through the howling
Storms of night
Just drifting
Fading into silence
Until nothing is left
But the quiet beating
Of an unheard heart.

Stolen Pieces

There aren't many pieces left now
Of this old broken heart
And though my love was always
Meant to be given away
I never anticipated
How much of it would be stolen.

Silence

You can never truly understand me
Until you've understood my silence
For it screams all my truths
Even as I lie to myself.

She had eyes that smiled. But oh, how her tears had another story to tell.

Into the Flames

She's the kind of girl
Who would walk
Through hellfire for you
But she's also the one
Who would throw you
Into those fiery flames
When you break her heart.

Ever After

She could never
Find the strength
To turn the page
Always fearful
And quite certain
Happily ever after
Only existed
In fairytales.

Cold of Winter

Autumn always reminds me of you, beautiful and vibrant, coloring my world in all my favorite hues. Then came the harsh cold, as I watched you fade away, drifting away on the bitter winds, taking all the colors with you, as I lay frostbitten, praying for some shelter from yet another desolate winter storm.

Loose Strings

I don't believe in
'No strings attached'
In the end
Those loose strings
Either wrap themselves
Around your unwilling heart
Or in a hangman's noose
Around your throat
As you struggle to breathe
Realizing that this time
They're not coming back.

All or Nothing

But oh the tragedy
Of being an
All or nothing
Kind of girl
Who could only ever
Have part of you.

Memories Within

There's music that breaks your heart
And then there's music that reaches
Way down deep into your soul
Pulling out every old memory
Every moment you begged to forget
And every heartbeat you ever skipped
The ones that remind you
That letting go was never an option.

Lost In Madness

Alice

Pray tell my darling Alice
How is it that you can see
Beyond the magic looking glass
That just looks right back at me
You disappear so often
Dear Alice where can you be
You're slaying all your demons
While madness joins you for your tea
You've been gone for quite a while
And you've beat the bloody queen
So it's time now to wake up
Dear Alice it's all just been a dream.

Finding Wonderland

She spent the rest of her life
Searching for Wonderland
Refusing to believe
It was all in her head
Hoping there was just enough
Magic left within herself
To get her back
To the only place
That she ever truly belonged.

Wonderland of Dreams

Take my hand
Let me show you what it's like
To fly through my
Wonderland of dreams
Drift away with me
Sailing through the stars
Until our hearts meet on the horizon
Of what's real, and what's not
Lay beside me
Beneath the wings of
Tomorrow's possibilities
And take comfort in the thought
That it was never a dream at all
For Wonderland is real
And it's waiting.

*I followed the white rabbit,
And you know what I found?
Myself.*

Extraordinary

The strength of her heart
Came from the madness
That bled from her soul
A Wonderland of chaos
Where extraordinary
Fell from a rabbit hole.

Forgotten Dreams

Once upon forgotten dreams
Nothing is what something seems
But there within she found her soul
Amidst the magic rabbit hole.

Sipping Tea

As Alice sat there sipping tea
She could taste just a touch of insanity
A hint of madness in every drop
And poor Alice drank the whole damn pot.

Curiouser

He saw Wonderland in her eyes
A touch of madness
A little bit lost
And a whole lot of magic
And down into Wonderland
        Deeply
      Madly
    He dove
Lost within
   Curiouser
     And
        Curiouser.

Beautiful Madness

He opened his heart
Long enough to see
Just how beautiful
Her madness could be.

Heart of Madness

There was nothing wrong with her mind
It was her heart that drifted to madness
As she fell way down into her Wonderland
While reaching for a cure to sadness.

Beyond Wonderland

My dreams don't
Take me to
Wonderland
They take me
To all the places
That lie just
Beyond it
Where not even
Alice
Dares to go.

My Home of Madness

Welcome to my madness
Where chaos is the norm
Happiness is playing
Checkers against my demons
The butterflies only
Come out at night
And fairytales always end
With the dragon
Enjoying their meal
It's not a beautiful place
But it's home.

One Last Adventure

She found Wonderland
When she needed it most
Just below the surface
Of who she thought she was
And barely above
Who she was destined to be
Where the heart and soul meet
For one last adventure
Of a lonely girl falling deep
So she can rise as the woman
She was always meant to be.

*My thoughts may be on the brink of madness,
but they all sound perfectly normal to me.*

Impossibly Possible

My dearest Alice
What secrets do you hold
What have the wildflowers whispered
Upon the midnight lull
Did they tell you why he grins
That clever Cheshire Cat
Or what magical madness lies
Within the Hatter's hat
My dearest Alice
Did you not know
The impossible possibilities
Beyond that rabbit hole
What a wonderous world
Living within your dreams
Where everything you see
Is nothing what it seems
So dream away, dear Alice
Imagination must be fed
Be careful though
While you're there
Not to lose your head.

Finding Peace

*Sometimes we have to let our dreams lead us
And have faith that they know the way.*

Lost

Lord I feel so lost right now
And I cannot find my way
The ones I thought meant so much
Were the ones who didn't stay
Lord please send me an angel
To help me get through today
To guide me down this road
Until again I find my way.

I Tried

Lord I hope you know I tried
To be more than who I am
I tried to give my everything
Hoping to proudly stand
But it's all just so hard sometimes
And I'm trying to not give in
I'm struggling to hold my ground
To not disappoint you again
Keep faith in me as I have you
That some day I will break free
And become the person that I should
So that you'll be proud of me.

*Everyone is so consumed with trying to figure out
who they are that they forget to question
who it is they want to be.*

Doubt

Just look at you girl, burning yourself out
Trying your hardest to erase your self doubt
Who made you believe you were anything less
Just who is it you think that you have to impress
You keep hurting yourself, but dear girl can't you see
You're already better than they thought you could be.

*We're all prisoners of our own mind's self deceit,
bound and shackled by the mere perception of limitations.*

For a Moment

The thought of you still lingers
Captivating my mind
All of the possibilities
That we just left behind
Things could have been so different
Had we met at another time
But still for that one moment
That one beautiful moment
You were mine.

*The only one who can silence the music in your
soul is you. Let it be your favorite song that
you play for all the world to hear.*

Embrace the Storm

Never be afraid of the coming storm.
Chase it. Embrace it. Become it.
Because a storm of your magnitude
Will have the ability to knock down everything
Standing in your way.

Rising Tide

The way I feel for you is like the rising tide
The waves come crashing, beating against my soul
Begging me to go swimming in the possibilities of you
So quickly the tide has risen and I have been swept away
Pulled under by your current, gasping for air to breath
And when the waves cast me back upon the rocky shore
I'll climb back to the ledge and jump in once more
Just to drown in you.

*You've spent so much time searching for the key
to happiness, that it never occurred to you
that the door was never locked in the
first place. All you had to do was open it.*

Rock Bottom

She hit rock bottom time and time again
Each time being judged, ridiculed
And condemned for never being good enough
Yet each time she climbed, again and again
Until she touched the stars and kissed the moon
And rock bottom became a distant memory
Not good enough to remember.

The Path Worth Taking

Not all paths are made of smooth cobblestone.
Often they are little more than a few broken boards
barely held together by rotten twine. They are
intimidating and scary as Hell. Do not look upon
this path with fear in your eyes. Take the challenge.
Assume the risk. If you can hold out just long enough
to get past it, you'll come to find that the most difficult
path to face will always be the one worth taking.

As The Bricks Fall

Sometimes all it takes is the right person pulling out the right
brick from the right place and the entire wall you've so
meticulously constructed around yourself will crash to the
ground. And maybe, just maybe, as those bricks fall, they'll
bury the demons you had imprisoned there with you, and
you will finally know what it feels like to be free.

Life necessitates change. It's impossible to move forward without the willingness to accept that change is inevitable, even if it means changing everything you are to become who you were meant to be.

Who You Are

Never worry about who they want you to be. Set your own standards. Raise your own bar. Push your own limits. But do it for you. Never for them. Always remember that their disappointment in you is nothing compared to the feeling you'll get when you look in the mirror one day and realize you've become someone you're not, all for the sake of someone's opinion. Choose your own path. Stick to your convictions. Have pride in who you become. Own it, because no one in this world deserves to own you.

Mosaic Masterpiece

Do not assume that I am broken. Maybe I have been before. And maybe, when I put the pieces back together, they may not have been put back how they were before, but they're all there in a marvelously intrinsic design that I laid out myself. A careful reconstruction of my soul. Yes, I have been broken before, but now I'm an epic masterpiece, created by the shards of my past. You see me as broken, but look closer, for I am truly a beautiful work of art.

*Sometimes my light may dim to a flicker,
But it still only takes a spark to light a wildfire.*

You're not just the song my heart dances to.
You're the whole damn symphony
And my soul is screaming for an encore.

A Train of Moments

Life is an endless train of moments, each linked together by various passenger cars. At each stop, some riders will exit and new passengers get on, and life continues until the next stop. And then sometimes, the train goes by so fast that we don't even have the opportunity to board, and that moment is gone. But although we may have missed our moment, that doesn't mean I won't be waiting for you at the next station. Look for me. I'll be there, determined not to miss the train again.

Play me the music of your soul,
And I will dance for you forever.

100% Authentic

To Hell with all the bullshit lies they feed you! It's a ridiculous notion that you should have to conform to society's expectations to be considered acceptable. Sorry society, but I wasn't built on an assembly line, and I don't need your Grade A stamp of approval, because the exceptional will never degrade themselves to being merely acceptable.

*Finally the pieces are all starting to fit together,
and though I cannot yet see the big picture, I know it's
going to be one Hell of a beautiful masterpiece.*

Flicker in the Dark

I know right now you feel like your life will never get better, and you've been praying for a light in your dark. That light you've so desperately been seeking is called hope, and at the moment, it's so dim that you can only occasionally make out a flicker. But it's still there. It hasn't left you or abandoned you. It sits there, in the dark with you, waiting for you to embrace it. So stand yourself back up and go to it. Hug the shit out of it, and don't let go this time. Fuel that little flicker of hope and watch the world light up with possibilities. Because life will get better, and the darkness will meet the dawn.

*Wisdom isn't about knowing the difference
between what you can and cannot change.
Wisdom is the knowledge that there is nothing you
cannot change if you are willing to work to change it.*

*If you settle for climbing half way up the mountain,
you'll never get the chance to experience all the beauty
that's been laid out for you at the top.*

Simple Things

Simple pleasures of simple love
So easily they are dismissed
Simple thoughts of simple hugs
Or the feeling of being kissed
Simply being held at night
And laying down beside you
The simple warmth of your soft touch
Heals me through and through
The simple feeling of your hand
Slipping between my fingers
The simple smell of your cologne
As through the air it lingers
Simple memories in my heart
Of the happiness you bring
And in a simple moment
Can simply mean everything.

Possibilities

Never before has anyone brought
My very soul to its knees
With little more than
The brief moment
Your eyes met mine
For in that moment
My soul wept
For the possibilities
Of all that we may become.

*Adapting to change
often necessitates
changing how you adapt.*

*I have never doubted how far I can go,
but rather how far anyone would go with me.*

Shining Bright

...And in that instant
When her eyes first met his
She knew
Never again would she
Face the darkness alone
Beside her
He would become
The only light
She ever needed
And my God
How brightly his light shone
Only for her to see.

*When you allow your spirit to be free,
your spirit will free you.*

*Of all the words, in all the languages,
not a single one of them can describe
just how much I love you.*

It Was You

Don't mistake my passion for lust
My passion was an outpouring of the
Intense emotions I felt for you
An overwhelming overflow of
What I was unable to self contain
It was never lust
But rather the manifestation
Of everything I wanted to say
But didn't
Everything I felt
But never told you
No, it wasn't lust
It was you
Just you.

Waiting For You

Reach into my heart
Until you hear my soul
Screaming your name
Then reach
Just a little bit further
That's where you'll find me
Waiting for you.

*If you shelter yourself from the storm,
you'll miss your chance to dance in the rain.*

Collision

And then, one day
All your stars
Collided with mine
Exploding with
Such an intensity
That even the gods
Took notice
And in that moment
The universe
Would never again
Be the same.

The Sound of Forever

How I've longed for
Such a moment
When time stands still
And the world fades away
When all that remains
Is the sound of our hearts
Beating to the rhythm
Of forever.

Resurrection

You reached into my soul
Lighting a fire in places
That have never felt warmth
Spreading your light where
I have only seen darkness
Resurrecting all that
I had forgotten existed
And waking a hope for life
That laid dormant for so long.

Just One Smile

I was so sure I never wanted
To see you again
But then, all it took
Was just one smile
For me to remember
All the reasons
That I did.

Crimson lips

Such sweet kisses from crimson lips
Magic dripping from those fingertips
Her touch so gentle, her heart so pure
She'll have you standing at Heaven's door
And before the night is done and through
Your heart will no longer belong to you.

*...And the greatest dream was found
within the smallest of opportunities.*

Fixer Upper

I've left the door to my heart open
In case you want to come in from the cold
There's a warm fire I've started for you
Waiting to melt the ice from your soul
It's a little bit of a fixer upper
But I've made it into a home
And I offer it to you, with open arms
So you'll never have to feel cold and alone.

To See You Smile

I see your heart, so heavy
Drowning in the ocean of sorrow
That she abandoned you in
Take my hand and let me
Guide you back to sunny shores
Rest your weary soul upon mine
And I will kiss away every scar
That she has inflicted upon it
Just hoping to see you smile
One more time.

Heaven

You were so busy
Looking at the beauty
Of the stars above you
To realize that Heaven
Was already standing
Right beside you.

Forever Home

I long for nights by the fireplace
I love you's whispered in my ear
Your warm touch upon my neck
Your fingers through my hair
I long for you to show me
The love I've never known
And be my forever and always
And always my forever home.

Envy

I saw you there
Standing in the rain
And I envied those drops
That touched your skin
And kissed your lips
As even the sky
Couldn't help but
To fall for you.

I Overcame

I've been shoved to my knees
I've been broken and shamed
I've been thrown under buses
And tossed into flames
My heart has been shattered
My soul has been stained
Yet I...
        I overcame

I rose from the ashes
I pushed back the pain
I've fought through the darkness
And my demons, I've slain
My scars all burn deep
And I'm not the same
Yet I...
        I overcame
              I overcame

Sailing Tides

Her heart carried her out to sea
Lost in a moment of drifting love
As the song in her soul carries her back
Sailing the tides of eternity.

Seek not the key to her heart,
For the key to her soul
Bears greater treasures.

Heart in a Jar

She lined the shattered pieces of her weathered heart along the cold tile floor, trying to match them together to resemble the heart she once believed could withstand the harshest storm. But this one shook her, deep within her bones. With so many damaged fragments, so many missing shards, it would never be whole again. So she swept them all up, placing them in a jar that she kept by the window, so the sun would catch them, spreading their radiance throughout the darkened room, to remind her that even broken, her heart still shined like Heaven.

Fragile

Touch me
Ever so gently
Delicately
For I am fragile
Trace me
With kind hands
Love me
The way you
Touch me
Never be afraid
To set me free
For I will always
Fly back to you.

Galaxies

Let me run my fingers down your back
And paint galaxies along your spine
Give me one night to touch your soul
And I'll let you make love to mine.

Breathless

And in that moment
When the sun kissed the moon
Night became day and day became night
And left breathless beneath satin sheets of stars
Heaven had fallen madly in love with the darkness.

Morning Coffee

You're the 4am thoughts
That linger in the taste
Of my morning coffee
Swirling in my mind
Spiraling, as I stir through
Last nights dreams
Slowly, my lips sip your
Smooth, sweet taste
And my, how I enjoyed
Every...
Last...
Drop.

Taste of Sin

I want the kiss that's so deep
My soul begs for mercy
And my lips tremble
For the taste of your sins.

Armored Heart

I wear a suit of armor
To protect my weary heart
In hopes that one day soon
You'll gently remove it all
From upon my heavy chest
Hiding my fragile heart
Forever within your soul.

Deep in my Veins

Your taste still rests upon my lips
Lingering, soaking deep into my skin
Coursing throughout all my veins
Burying it far within my soul
And instantly, I knew nothing
Would ever again be the same.

*Even the light is beautifully broken,
yet its warmth can be felt within your soul.*

Paper Stars

Be the kind of girl that still believes
In reading fairytales, dreams of magic
And makes wishes upon paper stars
For those are the ones who know
Happiness is only a chapter away.

Storybook Love

We all wanted that
Storybook kind of love.
We just never planned on
It becoming a tragedy.

To the Moon

If only we could sail to the moon
Catching stars along the way
Just to get lost within a kiss
Where the night embraces day.

*Sometimes the smallest acts of kindness
become someone's greatest blessing.*

Symphony

Every soul has its
Own song to play
But laying here
Next to you
I hear a symphony
And that's how I know
This is love.

Missed Moments

The journey not taken
Is a memory lost
Every missed moment
Comes at a cost
So give your heart
The blessing of trust
Before all that's left
Is ashes and dust.

Soft Heart Strong Spirit

May your heart be soft like summer rain
And your spirit as strong as a hurricane
Let your life be as full as the howling moon
And never let love be gone too soon.

Lost wishes are never truly lost, as they can always be found within your dreams.

Fine Wine

She tasted of
Sweet decadence
And elegance
A fine wine
Begging
To be sipped
Slowly
So slowly
By gentle lips
Of a noble
Connoisseur.

Wanting Heart

Your words touched me
In all the places
Your hands never could
Tracing across the edges
Of my wanting heart
Until even my soul
Lay naked and bare
Begging for more.

Fairytale Memories

Paint your children's dreams
With all the beautiful things
Unicorns, Fairies, pixie dust
Dragons, kings and queens
Fill their hearts with magic
Teach them to believe
Bless them with a childhood
Full of fairytale memories.

*Even in the harshest of conditions,
in loving hands, beautiful
souls will continue to grow.*

Raindrops and Roses

In a world where everyone
Wants to be a rose,
Be the raindrop that gives them
Strength to grow.

Heart's Desire

Meet me where the moon kisses stars
And old gypsy souls dance in fire
There I'll reveal my heart's intent
Within the flames of desire.

Resurrection

I Am She

I am not the mud you kick upon me.
I am not the stones of which you cast.
I am not the names you've given me,
Nor the shadows of my past.

I am she who stands with muddy bones,
Who built her castle from your stones,
She who rose above a life condoned,
And within my shadows, strongly grown.

I am she.
And I am not alone.

Words

I can turn every thought,
Every emotion, every feeling
Into pure poetry.
My words can make you cry,
Make you feel, make you strong.
I can turn my darkness to light,
My demons to angels,
And twist this craziness
Into something beautiful.
But do not ask me how it is I feel
As the words will escape
My very grasp every time.

*Sometimes we make sacrifices. Not because
we want to, but because we are strong
enough to accept that we have to.*

A Day to Rest

Yes. I'm tired. My body hurts, my mind is overwhelmed, and my soul is fucking exhausted. There are times when it gets absolutely unbearable and I'm pretty sure I'm going to collapse from it all. But I keep pushing and pushing in the hopes that a day will come when I can finally rest, knowing that I've accomplished becoming who I was meant to be. And no one can take that away.

Poetry of the Soul

Breathe your soul into mine
Wrap me in your truth
Tell me your darkest secrets
And I will fall for you
Hold on to me tightly
Promise to never let me go
Etch your words upon my heart
Write your poetry on my soul
And I will belong to you
Forever.

You wrote your words upon my heart
And gave me your soul to read.
In an instant, you became my favorite story.

The Dusty Book

I was nothing more than a dusty, forgotten book when you pulled me off the bottom shelf. All tattered and worn out, still, you thumbed your way through my pages, carefully turning each one, learning my story, one chapter at a time. And when you had finished the last one, to my surprise, you did not put me back on the shelf like so many had before. Instead, you wrapped me up in your arms and took me home, where you gave me a new place to belong and a whole new chapter to write.

Let It Burn

When it feels like everything's crashing and burning around you, your instinct will be to extinguish the flames. But let that fire rage. Let it all burn to cinders. Let it burn everything that is left, because when it's done, and the rains have washed away the ashes, you will no longer be bound to the abandoned, broken building that had confined you for so long. And from the ashes of that burnt down torment, you will rise again, stronger than ever before.

*The most difficult part of getting through
any struggle is convincing yourself that you can.*

A Woman Like Me

I will not beg. I will not plead.
I am far better of a woman
Than you give me credit to be
I am the one who will open their arms
To shelter you when you're in need
The one who will love you for your faults
And bring your demons to their knees
I can free you from your prison
And will forever aim to please
But do not ask me to beg for you
For I will not bow, simply to appease
This woman who stands in front of you
Is so much more than you can see
Yet all I wanted from you
Was just the opportunity
But no, I will not beg for it
When others would beg
For a woman just like me.

*We are all beautiful works of art.
We just interpret each other differently.*

*You can break me a thousand times. Again and again
I shall rise and turn it into something beautiful.*

Finding Peace

Cross into the dark forest
Come find me in the mist
Bring me all your demons
And I will lay them all to rest
Show me your very worst
And I'll show you my very best
Cry to me your sorrows
Then lay your head upon my chest
I will tame your darkest shadows
And leave the Devil himself impressed
And then return you to the light
To find your peace to rest.

Casted Away

I see the image of an angel in the clouds
And where her halo is supposed to be
I see a single beam of light
Shining its way through
Casting its glory upon an
Aristocratic cocktail party
Where they hide beneath
Umbrellas and awnings
On an otherwise cloudy day.

Rise Up

Rise up, little girl, the sun has not yet set
Go where you have not been
And meet who you have not met
Rise up, little girl, it's not yet time to rest
For the world lies in waiting
And you are truly blessed.

Dear God

Shine your grace upon me
By your Heavenly light
Cast away my demons
And give me strength to fight
Walk me through the shadows
And shield me from the pain
Help me to understand
The things I cannot explain
Guide me with your wisdom
When I should self deceive
Provide me with hope and faith
In all that I believe
Please take away my heartache
So that I may love again
Forgive me for all my lies
And wash away my sins
Hold me close within your arms
And take me by the hand
Bless me my dear Father
Until next to you I stand.

The key to succeeding at anything in life is to always expect more of yourself than anyone else ever possibly could.

Never Fade

When your struggles made you cry
I was there to wipe your tears
When you were too afraid to try
I would help you face your fears
I'm sorry I can't be there now
To tell you that it's alright
To walk you through this darkness
And be your guiding light
I will always stand beside you
Even when you cannot see
I'll look down upon you always
And always with you I will be
You'll have to wipe your tears this time
And you should never be afraid
I'm a part of you forever
As the memories will never fade.

Being strong isn't about not letting yourself be defeated. It's about being defeated. Owning that defeat and persisting forward. It's about knowing that defeat does not own you. So own it. Use it. Rise above it.

Little Blessings

Hush now, my sweet child
Whispers the summer breeze
Enjoy your flights of fancy
And doing what you please
Enjoy the little moments
Your heart tells you that it needs
Spend some time discovering
All the possibilities
The world is overwhelming
And can bring you to your knees
But sometimes we all forget
What a blessing it can be.

Warrior of Peace

She was a warrior of the gods
She fought with the strength
And wisdom of Athena
And loved with all the passion
And beauty of Aphrodite
Yet, her only desire was
To lay down her armor
Bury her sword in
A field of wildflowers
And live in the hope
Of finding peace and
Atonement within herself
If only the gods would
Allow her to be free.

Double Shot

I watch you sitting there, sipping your Bud Light,
That glimmer of mischief in your eyes,
And I know trouble's headed my way.
I resisted those charms time and time again,
But today I feel myself giving in.
So bartender, bring me a double shot,
Cause I won't be going home alone.
Trouble's finally won me over.

Gasoline

I'm dousing my yesterdays
In a gallon of gasoline
Lighting that match
And setting it on fire
Just so I can watch it
Burn to the ground
Cause it no longer matters
Who I was a day ago
A month ago
A year ago
When I become a different person
With every passing moment
So I'm going to light it up
And let it fade with it's ashes
Carried away on the
Inevitable winds of change.

Textationships

How did we go from holding hands and kissing lips
And all the beautiful things about relationships
To heart shaped emojis on profile pics
What happened to holding each other tight
And conversations held beneath the starry night
And that chill down your spine when they touch you just right
How can someone a thousand miles away
Wipe the tears from your cheeks on a bad day
Or hold you close and whisper 'it'll be okay'
So do not offer me empty textationships
I want all the realness of relationships
To feel the touch of your hand upon my hips
To feel the comfort of your embrace
And wake in the morning to see your face
Starting together another beautiful day
Because beside you will always be a more beautiful day.

Bandages and Battles

You can't bandage broken promises
And time won't heal your wounds
You can light that bridge on fire
But it may not burn for you
You can cast away your demons
And still not see the light
You can't avoid the battles
And still hope to win the fight
You can stand fast and hold your ground
To whatever comes your way
But never let them tell you
That you can't survive the day.

I rarely feel my own strength,
But when it really matters,
It never fails me.

Infinite

Made of moonlight and stardust
Her soul burned with the fire
Of a thousand suns
And infinite possibilities
And my, how she shone
Brightly upon the world.

You can leave your footprints across the sands of time,
but the winds of change will always seek to cover them.

Tequila Sunrise

I was not made of
Sugar and spice
Nor everything nice
But rather a
Perfect concoction
Of midnight moonlight
And tequila Sunrise.

*...And even Death saw
the beauty in life.*

These Wings

These wings were never strong enough
To fly among the angels
But they did soar through the clouds
And touch every single star
And if that's as close to Heaven
As I'll ever get, well then
That's good enough for me
For what a blessing it is to have been
Strong enough to fly at all.

Texas Honey

Your words were sweet
Like Texas honey
With the smooth burn
Of southern whiskey
Intoxicating me
Numbing me to
My bare soul
And I knew
One shot would
Never be enough
Of you.

*My soul dripped with ink from the
moment you made my heart bleed.*

Autumn Nights

How I long for cool, crisp nights,
Bathed in hues of orange and gold.
The sweet aroma of cinnamon
And cider filling the air.
Us, sitting together beside the fire,
Watching it dance away towards the stars,
As if carrying our wishes to the Heavens.
The sounds of crickets,
Singing their Autumn lullabies,
Soothing our hearts, as we drift away
Into an ocean of dreams,
Within each others arms,
Enchanted by the magic
Of Autumn nights.

Jumbled

Her ink was so diluted with tears
That the jumbled, blended words
That she had written on the page
Finally matched the jumbled
Blended words in her head
And it was the most beautiful
Poetry she had ever seen.

Poor Little Girl

Poor little girl, left broken and bruised,
Lonely, forgotten, and misunderstood,
The world passed by and left you for dead,
And never an apology ever was said.

Poor little girl, you deserved to be loved,
Not drowned in despair and shoved in the mud,
Not lonely, forgotten, nor misunderstood,
Nor bleeding your heart out onto the floor.

Poor little girl, I'm so sorry for you.
I've been where you are. I've walked in your shoes.
I've laid here before, sad and confused,
So I will not leave you broken and bruised.

Poor little girl, you are never alone.
It's not your time to be forgotten and gone.
So stand yourself up, dust yourself off,
And show this world that you're good enough.

Bits and Pieces

Some wings aren't
Made in Heaven
Some are made
Bit by bit
And piece by piece
By those who
Can see beauty
In what others would
Simply allow to
Whither away.

*You'll never learn to fly if you're
too afraid to break the cage.*

Tiny Wings

I never got to see your face
Or touch your soft, sweet skin
I never got to hold your hand
But I held you deep within
You took a piece of my heart
Along with you too
As to the Heavens, high above
On those tiny wings you flew.

*The subtlety of her silence
said everything.*

Blessed

Strength in her spirit
A song in her soul
Blessed is the woman
Who's wildly grown
Running with the wind
As far as she can go
Living free and loving life
For all that it bestows.

No matter how perfect life seems, there will always be days that your heart reminds you that life will never be perfect.

Blank Pages

So many nights she sat there
Writing her soul onto blank pages
Her heart dripping out
Through the ink of a pen
Tired and weary, she writes
Until stardust covers her eyes
And lullabies of sweet dreams
Fill in the end.

You weren't the poetry that I wrote, but rather the book that kept all my words from falling apart.

Free

Oh, for this soul to be free
It would fly to the Heavens
And sail across seas
It would dance with the stars
For the whole world to see
Oh, what it would be like
For this soul to be free.

Exquisitely Broken

She made broken look exquisite
Wearing her shattered soul
Upon the face of a warrior
Showing her scars with pride
Daring anyone to tell her
She's not strong enough to survive.

Angel Dust

Her soul was filled with magic
Her heart with moonlight dreams
Her beauty kissed by butterflies
And other wondrous things
She left a trail behind her
Just a bit of angel dust
A tiny blessing in the lives
Of every soul she touched.

Catching Stars

Should the stars rain down
I would catch them for you
Keeping them in a jar
Like summer fireflies
So that your wishes may come true
On your cloudiest days
And their shine will brighten
Even the darkest of nights.

Her tears turned to ink,
So she wrote them all free,
Turning all her pain into pure poetry.

Siren Song

She was the siren's deadly song
Singing of sensuality
Driving even the hardest men
Down upon their weary knees
Drowning them in her beauty
Tempting them as she pleased
Laying claim to what she wanted
Within the magic of the seas.

A Fairytale Fool

I played the fool well
In your fairytale
But I have my
Own story to write
Where I am the queen
And you are just my
Once upon a time.

Painted Wings

She sits there quietly in a haze
As those old memories begin to play
Of times forgotten within a dream
When she still flew on broken wings
And though she'll never grow them back
She wears them still, now painted black.

Unwritten Poetry

She wore her story proudly
Like a finely sewn dress
Her heart exposed
For the world to read
But for those who choose
To read her soul instead
Find beauty within the pages
Of her unwritten poetry.

The Beast Within

She was beauty and sin
With her own beast within
That hungered for fairytales
Soaked in vodka and gin.

Unstoppable

I am a good woman
A strong woman
Bowing to nothing
But my own morals
And beliefs
I fly highest
On the windstorms
Of a chaotic life
Daring the thunder
To roar louder than I
I am good
I am strong
I am unstoppable
And I am free.

Song in the Stars

There's music in her veins
And poetry in her soul
She's the song on the wind
Calling you to come back home
Her heart sings of solace
Comfort within her arms
The promise of forever
Written in the stars.

The Divine

Being broken is the easy part.
Piecing yourself back together
Without losing who you are,
That takes a great strength
That few will ever understand,
And that's okay.
For you, my dear,
Are a queen. A warrior. A goddess.
And the divine were never
Meant to be understood.

Road to Nowhere

All I need to find myself
Is music in my heart
Rhythm in my soul
And getting lost
On a long road
To nowhere.

*Beautiful is she whose soul bleeds color
into a world of black and white.*

Gypsy Soul

She was
Magic and madness
Heaven and sin
The angel above
The Devil within
A drifter
A dreamer
The stars in the sky
An old gypsy soul
That learned to survive.

Warrior

Being a warrior means
Fierceness of heart
Strength of Soul
And an unwavering
Willingness to fight
For your beliefs
Even if it means
Fighting alone.

True strength comes not from what the world sees,
But rather when you are alone,
Unable to pick yourself up,
And yet, somehow, you do.

Curtain Call

She dances across
Ballrooms made of stars
And stages bathed in tears
And oh, how the Heaven's wept
When her performance
Came to an end
And the curtain called
For the last time.

Do Not Grieve

Do not place flowers upon my grave
No need to cry or grieve today
I left my heart for you to hold
And many memories to be shared and told
So smile for me and please stay strong
For I'm home in Heaven
Where I belong.

Casting Light

She rose like the sun
Every single morning
Intending to cast her
Light upon someone's life
Even if only upon her own.

The Mark of a Queen

A true queen
Will have a crown
Tainted by warpaint
And soiled
By the ground
She desperately
Fought for.
She is not weak
Nor feeble
She is strong
Independent
And she will leave
Her mark
On this world.

Survival

For mine was a soul
Built strong and wild
Fiercely fighting
For my survival
The wolf inside
Howling to be free
The warrior heart
That made a
Woman like me.

*Glass slippers are irrelevant
To a girl who would rather
Be dancing in the pouring rain.*

Phoenix Fire

She was never meant
To be a summer flower
She is the dragon's breath
And the phoenix fire
A soul built of passion
Burning from within
Heaven's favorite angel
And the Devil's
Favorite sin.

Every Voice

My strength did not come
From every time I fell down
It came from every hand
That pulled me back up
And every voice
That whispered
You are not
Alone.

Beautifully Badass

Yes. I've wanted to give up so many times before.
But I'm still here. Still standing. Still fighting for a better me.
A better day. And though my legs tremble, and my soul is tired,
I shall keep trudging forward, through the fire and through the mud,
Until I find my peace to rest within a heart that refuses
To be anything less than beautifully badass.

Wolf Language

You can never hope to understand
A girl whose soul speaks
The language of wolves
As her heart runs wild and free
With a love too fierce and strong
For others to ever comprehend.

Warrior Brave

She didn't want to be brave anymore
But life had made her a warrior
And she no longer knew how
To be anything less than fierce
The wolf of the sheep
The queen of the kings
The dragon that would slay them all
To protect little more than
The heart they now tried to cage
No, she did not want to be brave
But life had made her a warrior
So that's who she was going to be.

Dedicated to my beautiful daughter, Haley-
My strength
My hope
My light in the dark.

From the Ashes
By Haley Crombie

I'll rise through the flames,
Through violence, ash and cinders.
My feathers whithered, tattered and torn.
My pride burnt and broken.

Yet I fight!

I will fight against their power.
I will fight against command.
I will fight for an eternity
For only then will I ascend.

Because only then...

My spirit can remain unbroken.
My faith cannot be shattered.
I cannot flee and I will not hide
Because I will always fight for what matters.

Social Media:

Please join me on Facebook:

CLS Poetry by Christie Starkweather

And on Instagram:

@clspoetry

Acknowledgements:

Thank you to all that have supported me through social media. I am very blessed for you all!

Special thanks to those who have walked this journey with me, encouraging me, motivating me, and believing in me:

*Haley Crombie, Fran & Alan Wohl,
Richard & Terrell Starkweather,
Bryon & Esequiel Cortez-Crombie,
Chris Henderson, Dawn Stull, Andrea Hatley,
Teresa Craig, Tina Guthrie*

Made in the USA
Coppell, TX
18 August 2020